POLICE
TECHNOLOGY
21ST-CENTURY CRIME-FIGHTING TOOLS

LAW ENFORCEMENT AND INTELLIGENCE GATHERING

POLICE
TECHNOLOGY
21ST-CENTURY CRIME-FIGHTING TOOLS

EDITED BY GLEN C. FORREST

Britannica®
Educational Publishing

IN ASSOCIATION WITH

ROSEN
EDUCATIONAL SERVICES

Published in 2017 by Britannica Educational Publishing (a trademark of Encyclopædia Britannica, Inc.) in association with The Rosen Publishing Group, Inc.
29 East 21st Street, New York, NY 10010

Distributed exclusively by Rosen Publishing.
To see additional Britannica Educational Publishing titles, go to rosenpublishing.com.

First Edition

Britannica Educational Publishing
J.E. Luebering: Executive Director, Core Editorial
Anthony L. Green: Editor, Compton's by Britannica

Rosen Publishing
Kathy Kuhtz Campbell: Senior Editor
Nelson Sá: Art Director
Brian Garvey: Designer
Cindy Reiman: Photography Manager
Bruce Donnola: Photo Researcher
Introduction and conclusion by Daniel E. Harmon

Library of Congress Cataloging-in-Publication Data

Names: Forrest, Glen C., 1953– editor.
Title: Police technology : 21st-century crime-fighting tools / edited by Glen C. Forrest.
Description: First edition. | New York, NY : Britannica Educational Publishing in association with The Rosen Publishing Group, 2017. | Series: Law Enforcement and Intelligence Gathering | Includes bibliographical references and index.
Identifiers: LCCN 2016020471 | ISBN 9781508103790 (library bound)
Subjects: LCSH: Police—Equipment and supplies—Juvenile literature. | Crime prevention—Technological innovations—Juvenile literature. | Police—Juvenile literature.
Classification: LCC HV7936.E7 P656 2017 | DDC 363.2/30284—dc23
LC record available at https://lccn.loc.gov/2016020471

Manufactured in China

Photo credits: Cover, pp. 3, 82 John Moore/Getty Images; pp. 8–9, 46 Portland Press Herald/Getty Images; pp. 8–9 (background), 12, 29, 53, 67 hunthomas/Shutterstock.com; p. 13 Courtesy of the New York City Police Department; p. 18 © ADS/Alamy Stock Photo; pp. 20–21 Print Collector/Hulton Archive/Getty Images; pp. 24–25 © Bob Daemmrich /Alamy Stock Photo; p. 28 Pacific Press/LightRocket/Getty Images; pp. 30–31 Benoit Daoust/Shutterstock.com; p. 36 Andreas Solaro/AFP/Getty Image; pp. 38–39 Adrian Dennis/AFP/Getty Images; p. 44 Paul Buck/EPA/Newscom; p. 48 Matt Cardy/Getty Images; p. 51 © AP Images; p. 55 Kevork Djansezian/Getty Images; p. 57 © Stockbyte/Thinkstock; p. 60 Science & Society Picture Library/Getty Images; pp. 64–65 Boris Roessler/picturealliance/dpa/AP Images; pp. 68–69 Allen J. Schaben/Los Angeles Times/Getty Images; p. 70 Pool/Getty Images; p. 72 Scott Camazine/Alamy Stock Photo; p. 75 © kpzfoto/Alamy Stock Photo; p. 78 © Greg Sorber/Albuquerque Journal/ZUMA Press; pp. 80–81 BSIP/Newscom; pp. 86–87 BSIP/Universal Images Group/Getty Images; p. 88 Odd Andersen/AFP/Getty Images; p. 89 Drew Angerer Getty Images; pp. 90–91 George Frey/Getty Images; back cover, interior pages (background) stefano carniccio/Shutterstock.com

CONTENTS

INTRODUCTION

Police technology encompasses the wide range of scientific and technological methods, techniques, and equipment used in policing. As science has advanced, so too have the technologies that police rely on to prevent crime and apprehend criminals. Police technology was recognized as a distinct academic and scientific discipline in the 1960s, and since then a growing body of professional literature, educational programs, workshops, and international conferences has been devoted to the technological aspects of police work.

Many examples of an incipient police technology date from ancient and medieval times. For example, the ancient Egyptians used detailed word descriptions of individuals, a concept known in modern times as *portrait parlé* (French: "spoken portrait"), and the Babylonians pressed fingerprints into clay to identify the author of cuneiform writings and to protect against forgery. Nevertheless, early technology was quite crude, such as the medieval methods of trial by ordeal and trial by combat, in which the innocence of suspects was established by their survival. A more humane medieval method, and a step toward modern concepts, was compurgation, in which the friends and families of a disputant took oaths not on the facts but

A Scarborough, Maine, police officer views an image from a thermal imaging camera after making a traffic stop. Officers need to stay informed about technological developments to enhance their law-enforcement work.

on the disputant's character. Formalized police departments were established in the late seventeenth century in continental Europe, and since that time technologies have developed rapidly—transforming police work into a more scientific endeavor.

Yet police technology differs greatly in type and sophistication from country to country. It is generally more sophisticated in countries that are wealthy and that produce or import a high level of technology. (However, undemocratic countries tend to invest a great share of their gross national product in police technology, even when they are poor.) Police technology also depends on the physical setting and the political environment where police work is done. Urban policing relies more on technology than small-town and rural policing, and the degree to which a police force is militarized has a strong impact on its weaponry. Finally, some newer crimes, such as cybercrime, can be fought only by using an extensive array of technology that exceeds the scope of police technology proper.

This volume reviews advances in police mobility, from the earliest foot patrols to aerial pursuit and surveillance, and in communication, from the first police telephone and radio systems to computer-assisted dispatch technology. It describes modern weaponry, including nonlethal chemical and electronic devices, and protective gear.

Computers and other electronics have become vital for police work in the twenty-first century. Applications explored in the book include the capability of searching extensive, internationally synchronized criminal information databases; plotting crime incidents and patterns to anticipate and prevent recurrences; interrogating criminal suspects and persons of interest; and identifying suspects by using such innovations as biometrics. New electronics technology has equipped police forces to conduct more effective audio and visual surveillance.

The volume also explains modern tools and techniques for collecting and analyzing crime scene evidence. Police organizations today employ forensic scientists and specialists such as toxicologists, serologists, botanists, and handwriting and document examiners to help resolve investigations.

Criminals in the internet age are using technology to carry out crimes with alarming new levels of sophistication. Police are responding with impressive technological weapons and tactics of their own.

CHAPTER ONE

POLICE TOOLS AND TECHNIQUES

I nventions and innovations have changed society dramatically over the centuries. They have proved especially beneficial to police. Technology has introduced new vehicles to improve the mobility of officers. It has advanced the techniques by which police forces communicate for daily operations. Steady progress in computer technology has also given agencies new systems for accumulating and managing criminal information.

MOBILITY

To be effective, police forces must be in close proximity to the citizens they serve. The first and most basic means of maintaining that close contact was the foot patrol. Officers were deployed by time of day (watches) and area (beats). Beats were kept geographically small to allow officers to respond to incidents in a timely manner. In larger rural jurisdictions, officers were deployed on horseback. Both foot and mounted patrols continue

Officers of the New York Police Department have various means of transportation for patrolling the city.

to be used throughout the world. Foot patrol is used in congested urban areas, in high-density housing complexes, and at special events; mounted patrol is also used for special events and for crowd control.

Foot and mounted patrols were followed by bicycle patrol, which spread throughout continental Europe at the end of the nineteenth century. Bicycle patrol made a comeback in the late twentieth and early twenty-first centuries as a compromise between foot and car patrols. Bicycle patrol officers are specially trained and equipped with robust but lightweight urban bicycles. Bicycles are very useful for patrolling urban parks, housing complexes, school campuses, and locations where there are multiple large walkways not immediately accessible from the street.

The development of the automobile in the late nineteenth century dramatically transformed police work in the early twentieth century. The city of Akron, Ohio, claims to have deployed the first automobile police patrol wagon in 1899. The vehicle was powered by an electric battery, however, which greatly limited its range over distances. A motorcycle patrol was instituted in New York City in 1905. By 1910 in France, twelve regional mobile brigades of police had become fully motorized; they used gasoline-powered automobiles manufactured by the De Dion-Bouton company to crisscross France. The motorization of police forces took place simultaneously in virtually all Western countries; by World War I, many urban police departments were using motorized patrols. Automobiles allowed police to expand patrol beats and reduced the time required for responding to incidents. However, the mobility and speed that police cruisers provided came at the expense of police visibility, as officers were increasingly encapsulated in their cars.

The police cruiser played a bigger role in the cities of the New World—Australia, Canada, New Zealand, and the United States—than elsewhere. New World cities generally were laid out in a gridlike pattern with large intersecting avenues that facilitated motorized police patrols. By contrast, European cities typically featured a maze of small, crowded streets that required foot patrols. The equipment carried by the standard police vehicle in these New World cities significantly evolved from the 1970s to the early twenty-first century. In the 1970s, the police car was basically the same as the mass-produced vehicles owned by citizens. It was fitted with few accessories for enhancing comfort, such as air conditioning, and the specific police equipment that it carried consisted of a two-way radio with limited capacities and an external rotating light fitted on its roof; a metal screen between the front and the back seats was common but not standard. By the twenty-first century, the modern big-city patrol vehicle was routinely fitted with heavy-duty alternators to power numerous electronic devices and a powerful cooling system to handle engine heat while idling during hot weather. It was also equipped with an array of electronic devices, including radios, siren and light controls, a public-address system, a cellular telephone, a radar unit to measure motorists' speed, and, in many jurisdictions, a mobile digital terminal for access to police databases. Even the trunk was filled with equipment, such as first-aid and biohazard-response kits. Like the police vehicle itself, such equipment reflects the technologies produced by domestic industries. In countries whose industrial sectors are large and technologically advanced, such as the United States, Germany, and Japan, police cruisers tend to be very sophisticated instruments; elsewhere, they are more rudimentary.

The array of duties performed by police today requires a variety of different vehicles, ranging from minicars to buses and fully equipped mobile headquarters. For example, traffic-law enforcement is often conducted by patrol officers on motorcycles, but cars are also commonly used. In the United States, police often drive sport-utility vehicles (SUVs) for highway patrol. Police cruisers are generally smaller in Europe and Japan than in the United States and Canada, reflecting the standards of domestic auto industries. In Germany and Italy, police may use sophisticated sports cars, such as Porsches, BMWs, and even Ferraris, for high-speed chases.

Some police vehicles have been adapted from military vehicles. The Police Service of Northern Ireland (formerly the Royal Ulster Constabulary), for example, has used military vehicles in its patrols. In the United States, some police departments have converted armored scout vehicles to assist in high-risk operations. Vehicles built on large chassis can be used to transport a fully equipped command center to a crime scene or disaster area.

The environment is another factor that determines the types of vehicles used by police forces. In many rural jurisdictions, the typical four-door sedan has been replaced by SUVs and four-wheel-drive trucks. In areas where there are no paved roads (such as open country, beaches, and forests), the police use all-terrain vehicles and off-road motorcycles. Snowmobiles and tracked vehicles are used in areas where large snow accumulations are typical.

Police departments that patrol waterfronts employ small to midsize open-cockpit motorboats. Customs and border-surveillance agencies have access to some of the most complex and exotic watercraft to combat illicit drug-running and border incursions. In areas with large swamps, the police use airboats (flat-bottomed boat hulls with an aircraft engine and propeller for propulsion).

Various types of aircraft are used in police patrols as well. Helicopters, the most common type, are often equipped with a high-intensity spotlight that can provide overhead illumination for units on the ground. Another

The New York Police Department has an aviation division that includes helicopters for assisting in personnel transport, firefighting, port security, and rescue operations, among other tasks.

device used by aircraft, a passive infrared unit sometimes called forward-looking infrared (FLIR), provides night vision. FLIR units can measure the heat energy emitted by objects and living things, enabling ground units to be directed to a particular location. The police also employ fixed-wing aircraft for operations such as border patrols and drug surveillance, police-personnel transport over long distances, and highway traffic control. They range in size from single-seat planes to multiengine jet aircraft.

COMMUNICATION

The vehicles discussed here would be nothing more than efficient conveyances if police officers were unable to communicate instantly with each other and the public. In the earliest police forces, communication was accomplished through oral or written orders in an administrative chain of command. As society progressed, the military was used less for domestic peacekeeping. Depending on whether a country evolved toward more or less centralization, systems of national or local control were established. In England, the watch-and-ward system evolved to provide citizens with protection from crime. During times of duress, the men on watch would raise the hue and cry to summon assistance from the citizens of the community or, in the case of a larger community, from others already on watch. The watch standers were equipped with various signaling devices, including bells and rattles.

With the passage of the Metropolitan Police Act in 1829, the police in England were formalized into a full-time paid service, as they had been in France, Austria, and Prussia. The system was directed by a central command through face-to-face contact between supervisors and subordinates. As urban areas expanded and the police were deployed to more beats over larger geographic areas, this system of human communication became increasingly inefficient. Face-to-face contact gave way to the use of telegraphs in the mid-nineteenth century, and in the late 1870s, police departments began installing telephone systems. In urban jurisdictions, call boxes, or street telephones, were placed on beats to enable patrol officers and citizens to alert the central command of disturbances. In 1937, the first emergency telephone system was established in London, where callers could dial 999 to speak to an operator.

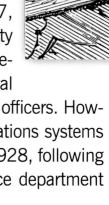

Early systems of police dispatch involved a single operator who took calls from the public and dispatched officers via radio. In 1917, the police department of New York City began equipping patrol vehicles with a one-way radio receiver that enabled the central command to send emergency messages to officers. However, that and other early radio-communications systems were fraught with technical problems. In 1928, following several years of experimentation, the police department

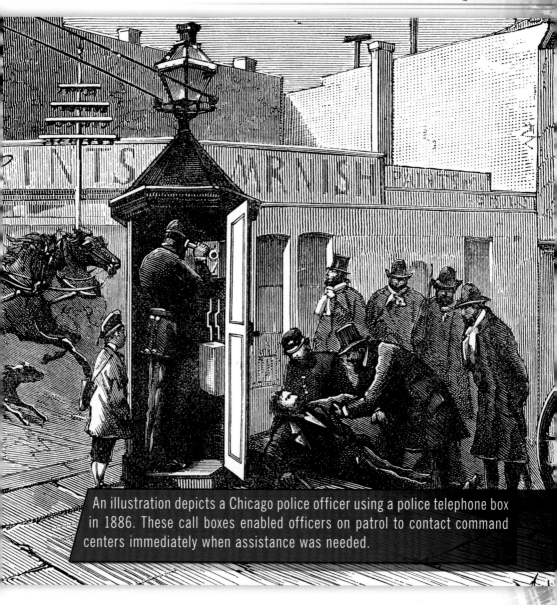

An illustration depicts a Chicago police officer using a police telephone box in 1886. These call boxes enabled officers on patrol to contact command centers immediately when assistance was needed.

of Detroit, Michigan, improved the technology to allow regular contact between headquarters and patrol units; the system developed in Detroit was subsequently the basis of police communications systems used throughout

FIRSTNET

Police already use body and dashboard cameras to record visual evidence during pursuits, investigations, and arrests. But law enforcers and other first responders—firefighters and emergency medical professionals—believe they could work more effectively if they were able to share live images and video, combined with voice communications, while situations are developing. Data could be streamed to and from command centers and responders on the scene and en route.

A government initiative that might make that possible is FirstNet, the First Responder Network Authority. A congressional act authorized the creation of FirstNet in 2012. It is an independent authority within the National Telecommunications and Information Administration, which is part of the US Department of Commerce. Implementation of FirstNet will be some years in the future; as of 2016, the network is still in the planning stage.

FirstNet will be an LTE (long-term evolution) network. LTE is a fairly recent type of wireless communications network. It can transmit large volumes of data over great distances at high speed.

On the FirstNet website (http://www.firstnet.gov), FirstNet administrators point out, "Situational awareness during an incident will help protect people, property and first responders. When public safety personnel have a common picture of an incident that's unfolding, they are far better equipped to respond."

FirstNet will stream real-time photos and video of emergency scenes. It will also report the locations of responders at the site and in the area. Eventually, developers hope to incorporate even more advanced technologies, such as an audio function that can pinpoint sources of gunfire.

FirstNet officials explain that the system will give local command centers greater ability to manage emergency situations. At the same time, it will integrate with regional and national operations centers as needed. In short, FirstNet is foreseen as "a single platform for public safety communications."

the United States. Two-way radio receivers were first deployed in 1933 in Bayonne, New Jersey, and their use proliferated in the 1940s. Radios in patrol cars were eventually supplemented by portable radio transceivers carried by individual officers to allow uninterrupted radio contact between officers and the dispatch center. Dispatch was improved in the United States in the late 1960s with the establishment of the 911 emergency telephone system. Similar systems have since been adopted in other countries throughout the world.

Police radio-communications systems benefited from the development of computers, which made possible the quick retrieval of information on stolen property, wanted persons, and other police intelligence. Computers were eventually placed in patrol cars. These mobile digital terminals (MDTs) enable officers to check licenses, wanted-persons lists, and warrants from the patrol vehicle without making an oral radio transmission. MDTs have been supplemented with a wide variety of digital pagers and cellular phones.

COMPUTERIZATION

The police were early adopters of computer database technology. In the United States, the National Crime Information Center (NCIC) was established in 1967; police records were subsequently computerized and made available to police agencies throughout the country. The NCIC's database enables local police departments to apprehend offenders who might otherwise evade capture. The database contains fingerprints, a registry of sexual offenders, and mug shots, and it can be queried for detailed information on stolen vehicles and warrants for firearms violations; it can even search for phonetically similar names. Similar databases maintained by US states provide police with access to misdemeanor warrants, driver-citation records, and vehicle-ownership information.

The European Union (EU) established a computerized information system—the Schengen Information System (SIS)—which allows the authorities of certain member states, plus some other European countries, to send or

While stopped in his patrol car, a Texas police officer speaks on his phone and types information into his mobile digital terminal (MDT). The MDT enables quick retrieval of vehicle records, arrest warrants, and other computerized information.

receive data about criminals, missing persons, stolen property, and other matters of interest to law enforcement officers. Each member of the EU, however, must devise its own computerized system to connect to the SIS. The European Police Office (Europol) also maintains a computerized database. In addition, Interpol manages databases of fingerprints, DNA (deoxyribonucleic acid) profiles, and information on stolen property and other matters, which member countries can retrieve through a global police- communications system known as I-24/7.

Computer-assisted-dispatch (CAD) systems, such as the 911 system in the United States, are used not only to dispatch police quickly in an emergency but also to gather data on every person who has contact with the police. Information in the CAD database generally includes call volume, time of day, types of calls, response time, and the disposition of every call. The Enhanced 911 (E911) system, adopted in the United States, instantly identifies the number of the phone from which the call is made, as well as the name and physical address of the person who owns the phone. Data maintained in the E911 system sometimes include a history of calls to the police from the caller's location. When the CAD system is linked to a global positioning system (GPS), dispatchers can immediately identify the police cruiser nearest the scene of the emergency.

Although records are essential for effective police operations, police departments would be overwhelmed

COMPSTAT

In the late twentieth century, police agencies and departments throughout the United States and in some areas of Britain began adopting computerized systems, known as CompStat (computerized statistics), that could be used to plot specific incidents of crime by time, day, and location. By revealing previously unnoticed patterns in criminal activity, CompStat enabled police departments to allocate their resources more effectively, and it was credited with significant decreases in crime rates in several of the cities in which it was used. CompStat became so widely used (in the United States) that many police administrators began to regard it as the basis of a new model of policing for the twenty-first century.

without a mechanism for filtering information and making sense of it. Police have long been able to gather information from related cases by using whatever records were available to them, but, until the advent of computerized databases, such cases could be found only through the recollection of experienced investigators. Computerized records systems can be extremely effective in drawing out relationships between past and present cases and suspects. The computer acts like a seasoned detective with an encyclopedic memory. Systems

Mayor Bill de Blasio of New York City watches a display of the CompStat system in the Joint Operations Center, a high-tech crime-fighting center. In 2016, New York unveiled a new version of CompStat that enabled the police department to share crime information with the public.

known as CompStat, used by a variety of large cities, enable police departments to piece together information and to deploy personnel efficiently.

CHAPTER TWO

EQUIPMENT
AND TACTICS

Until the late nineteenth century, many police officers worked in civilian clothes, especially in small towns and rural counties. In some cities, most officers were armed only with wooden nightsticks, also known as billy clubs. If they could not subdue a criminal on the streets single-handedly, they blew a shrill whistle to summon help.

Today, uniformed police typically carry an assortment of sophisticated weapons and defensive gear. They are highly trained in the use of each instrument and in personal confrontation tactics. Patrol and investigative officers are aided greatly by modern surveillance technology.

PERSONAL EQUIPMENT

Police officers, whether plain-clothed or uniformed, carry a variety of equipment with them on service calls. Police in uniform carry much more equipment than those in plain clothes, and members of special operations teams, such as SWAT and crowd-control units, carry even more, sometimes including full body armor complete with helmet, leg pads, and shield.

The amount of equipment carried by uniformed officers has grown considerably since the 1950s, when it basically consisted of a handgun in a holster, handcuffs, and a nightstick. The holster was attached to a Sam Browne belt—a wide belt, usually made of leather, supported by a strap extending diagonally over the right shoulder. The belt was ill-adapted to changes in other police equipment, however, and its use declined in the late twentieth century. Today, the belts worn by uniformed police officers in urban North America typically have a number of holsters or cases for carrying an automatic pistol, spare clips of ammunition, metal and plastic handcuffs, a portable radio, pepper spray, a collapsible baton, and

Police in riot gear protect a street in Montreal, Canada. Officers assigned to riot control typically wear helmets and full body armor.

a video microphone transmitter (if the officer's car contains a camera). A clipboard with spare report forms is also standard equipment. In addition, many police officers carry first-aid kits and other medical equipment, such as a defibrillator, in their patrol cars; they also may carry a portable breath analyzer (also called a Breathalyzer) for testing drivers who may be intoxicated. To this basic equipment many police officers add cell phones or pagers, flashlights, binoculars, tape recorders, portable scanners, plastic gloves, and extra weapons (for example, a spare gun, a confiscated knife, a blackjack, or brass knuckles). The practice of bearing extra weapons, being of questionable legality, is mostly done secretly, making it difficult to assess how extensive it is. However, it has been acknowledged by most police researchers. Finally, an essential piece of equipment is the bulletproof vest, which covers the torso of the officer and is worn either over or under the uniform shirt. Many such vests are made with the fiber Kevlar, which is capable of stopping most handgun projectiles and many types of knives. More robust vests, made of ceramic and fiber combinations that can withstand rifle fire, are used in bomb-disposal operations.

The quantity and diversity of equipment carried by police officers naturally depend on the financial resources allocated to police forces. North American police forces are generally better equipped than police forces in most other parts of the world; indeed, their equipment levels tend to be treated as benchmarks that other forces try to meet. Nevertheless, with the important exception of firearms, police equipment throughout the world is becoming increasingly standardized.

BULLETPROOF VEST

A bulletproof vest is a protective covering worn to protect the torso against bullets.

Metal body armor fell into disuse in the sixteenth and seventeenth centuries, partly because armor that was effective against bullets was too heavy to be practical. Modern body armor reappeared on a small scale in World War I as a means of protecting the torso from shell fragments, but the armor, as designed, was too heavy to justify the protection that it afforded. World War II stimulated the development of lighter body armor that consisted of overlapping plates of steel, aluminum, or bonded fiberglass attached within a nylon garment that covered both the front and the back of the wearer. These "flak jackets" were flexible enough to permit relatively free movement by the wearer while affording him adequate protection against shell fragments. They could not stop an armor-piercing bullet, however.

In the 1960s, new types of vests were developed whose plates were made of composite layers of steel or a very hard ceramic, boron carbide. However, the discovery that numerous layers of nylon fabric could dissipate the energy of a bullet revolutionized the use of modern body armor.

The function of steel or hard plastic armor is to be impervious to a bullet. By contrast, the textile vest deforms the bullet and then dissipates its energy, entangling it in the vest's many layers. A textile bulletproof vest is fashioned

(continued on the next page)

(continued from the previous page)

of sixteen to twenty-four layers of nylon cloth of a heavy weave, the layers stitched together like a quilt. Any ordinary pistol or submachine-gun bullet striking such a garment is immediately flattened as it hits the outermost layers, and the now mushroom-shaped slug dissipates its energy as it presses against the remaining thicknesses of the vest, unable to penetrate its overlapping layers of coarse mesh. The wearer of such a vest is usually bruised by the impact of a bullet, but without serious consequence. Vests of sixteen layers will stop regular handgun and submachine-gun bullets; those of twenty-four layers will stop the more powerful magnum bullets from the same weapons.

Apart from the obvious military applications of the fabric bulletproof vest, the rise of terrorism in the second half of the twentieth century led to the increased use of body armor by police and antiterrorist troops.

ARREST-AND-CONTROL TECHNOLOGIES AND TECHNIQUES

Firearms and clubs are only part of the equipment used in law enforcement today. Numerous other tools and methods enable officers to resolve incidents safely and effectively, usually without resorting to armed force.

NONLETHAL TACTICS AND INSTRUMENTS

Police officers routinely arrest suspects in the course of their duties. Although most suspects surrender without incident, some resist being taken into custody. In most such cases, police are able to subdue the suspect by using unarmed techniques, some of which are drawn from various martial arts (such as judo and aikido) or are based on knowledge of nerve pressure points.

Nonlethal weapons include electronic devices, chemical agents, and a variety of different striking instruments, such as straight, side-handle, and collapsible batons and an array of saps, truncheons, and clubs. The nightstick carried by police officers was originally made of wood, but most now are made of composite materials.

The straight baton, known as a nightstick or billy club, ranges in length from twelve to thirty-six inches (thirty to ninety centimeters). Because it is smooth and can be held from either end, it tends to inflict few cuts or lacerations; it can be used for both striking and control tactics. Additional features of modified batons may include a built-in flashlight, an electric charge, or a syringe (for administering an antidote to nerve gas, for example).

Electronic technologies include the stun gun, which delivers an electric charge that causes muscle spasms, pain, and incapacitation, and the TASER (a registered trademark), a type of electronic control device that fires two barbed projectiles that deliver an electric charge without requiring the officer to come within arm's reach of the suspect. Stun-gun technology is a good illustration of the globalization of police equipment. Most police forces that can afford nonlethal electric weaponry have invested in it—including those that resist the use of firearms.

Tear gas is traditionally used to disperse large crowds. Early aerosol sprays were used only sparingly because they vaporized quickly and could affect officers and

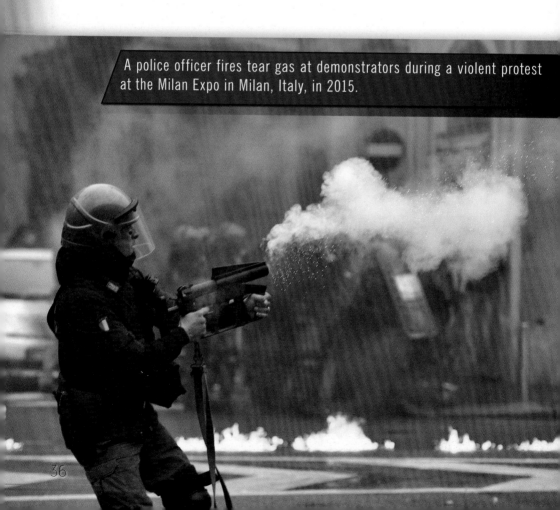

A police officer fires tear gas at demonstrators during a violent protest at the Milan Expo in Milan, Italy, in 2015.

TEAR GAS

Tear gas is a substance that irritates the mucous membranes of the eyes, causing a stinging sensation and tears. Tear gas may also irritate the upper respiratory tract, causing coughing and choking. It was first used in World War I in chemical warfare, but since its effects are short-lasting and rarely disabling, it came into use by law-enforcement agencies as a means of dispersing mobs, disabling rioters, and flushing out armed suspects without the use of deadly force.

The substances most often used as tear gases are synthetic organic halogen compounds. They are not true gases under ordinary conditions but are liquids or solids that can be finely dispersed in the air through the use of sprays, fog generators, or grenades and shells. The two most commonly used tear gases are 1-chloroacetophenone, or CN, and 2-chlorobenzylidene malononitrile, or CS. CN is the principal component of the aerosol agent Mace and is widely used in riot control. It affects chiefly the eyes. CS is a stronger irritant that causes burning sensations in the respiratory tract and involuntary closing of the eyes, but its effects wear off more quickly, after only five to ten minutes of breathing fresh air. Other compounds used or suggested as tear gases include bromoacetone, benzyl bromide, ethyl bromoacetate, xylyl bromide, and bromobenzyl cyanide. The effects of tear gases are temporary and reversible in most cases. Gas masks with activated charcoal filters afford good protection against them.

others in close proximity to the suspect—particularly inside a squad car. Sprays containing capsicum oleoresin, an irritant derived from pepper plants, proved to be more effective than other aerosols, and they possessed the additional advantage of being nonvaporizing.

For high-risk operations and crowd control, various irritating chemicals can be delivered by a handheld low-yield burst grenade, shotgun, or grenade launcher. The less-harmful PepperBall, which combines a compressed-air launcher and a projectile filled with capsicum oleoresin, was developed in the 1990s. Because the projectiles break upon impact, they usually do not cause permanent injury, even when fired at close range. The so-called beanbag projectile, which can be fired from shotguns and grenade launchers, contains a weighted flexible filler within a soft fabric pouch. Other nonlethal weapons include devices that use sound, light, or heat to cause confusion, pain, or temporary blindness.

POLICE DOGS

Dogs were first trained for police work at the turn of the twentieth century in Ghent,

Belgium, and the practice was soon adopted elsewhere. Although certain breeds with especially keen senses have been used for special purposes—such as detecting caches of illegal drugs and explosives and tracking

Officers In Copenhagen, Denmark, use police dogs to help restrain protesters. German shepherds, for example, are very capable as police dogs, search-and-rescue dogs, and military dogs because of their intelligence, alertness, and loyalty.

fugitives and missing persons—the most widely trained dog for regular patrol work is the German shepherd or Alsatian. Other breeds that are sometimes used include boxers, Doberman pinschers, Airedale terriers, Rottweilers, schnauzers, and bloodhounds. For detection tasks, the size of the animal is less important than its sense of smell. Selected animals must meet specific criteria regarding physical characteristics and temperament, and their training is comprehensive and rigorous.

FIREARMS AND EXPLOSIVES

Although police forces commonly authorize their officers to possess firearms and to use them when necessary, not all police carry these lethal weapons. There are four distinct cases in respect to the use of firearms by police.

First, there is the case of most police forces in the world: police officers carry firearms and are instructed to make minimal use of them. The number of police-caused fatalities varies greatly among such countries, the highest number being recorded in the United States.

Second, there are military police forces that are heavily armed with automatic rifles and submachine guns, such as the AK-47 used in countries in the Middle East, Asia, and other regions. Military police operate in most developing countries, where civilian police forces are typically underfunded and undertrained. Although many governments consider the use of heavy weapons by police to be justified by the threat to society posed by dangerous criminals, critics have claimed that heavily armed police tend to kill large numbers of people unnecessarily, sometimes in circumstances that amount to extrajudicial execution. In the Brazilian state of São Paulo, for example, military police shot and killed hundreds of people each year in the late twentieth and early twenty-first centuries in what were officially reported as shoot-outs with criminals.

Third, there are some police forces that do not carry firearms in any circumstances. Such police operate in the cities of continental Europe under the local authority of a mayor. Unarmed, they perform various order-maintenance duties, such as the enforcement of local bylaws and traffic regulations.

Finally, a small number of police forces severely restrict the use of firearms by their personnel. Today, police officers do not normally carry firearms in New Zealand, Norway, Iceland, and the United Kingdom (except in Northern Ireland, where officers of the Police Service of Northern Ireland are armed). In New Zealand, only the members of Armed Offenders Squads (AOS), which were established in 1964 after the fatal shooting of four police officers, are allowed to carry and use firearms. Each AOS is staffed with part-time police volunteers drawn from all branches of the police, and the squads operate only on a call-out basis. In Norway, only a police chief can authorize the use of firearms by officers, and in Iceland police are unarmed during routine patrols partly because of the belief that arming officers with firearms leads to more gun violence than it stops. In the United Kingdom, officers are allowed to use firearms only in specific circumstances. In England and Wales, as in other countries, restrictions on the use of firearms by police have helped to minimize the number of unintended fatalities resulting from police operations. Nevertheless, after a series of terrorist bombings in the London public transportation system in 2005, there were calls in Britain for increasing the number of police officers authorized to use firearms.

HANDGUNS, SHOTGUNS, AND RIFLES

The first practical police firearm, the multishot revolver, was patented in 1835 by Samuel Colt. In the 1850s, the British gun manufacturer Beaumont-Adams introduced the self-cocking double-action revolver. In contrast with the Colt, which needed to be cocked before firing, the double-action revolver could be fired by just a direct pull on the trigger. This allowed for quicker fire, at the expense of precisely aimed shots. In the United States and throughout the British Empire, the double-action revolver became, with few exceptions, the police sidearm of choice for more than a century.

Semiautomatic pistols were developed in Germany in the late nineteenth century by Peter Paul Mauser, whose Mauser rifle became a standard infantry weapon. In 1911, the .45-caliber single-action semiautomatic pistol developed by the American weapons designer John Browning was adopted by the US military. Yet despite the advent of semiautomatics, double-action revolver pistols remained important police weapons not only for their capacity for quick firing; they also were perceived as more reliable than semiautomatics, whose firing mechanism tended to jam. In addition, double-action pistols were more secure than semiautomatics, as it took a significant amount of pressure on the trigger to fire them. Nevertheless, semiautomatics had more firing power and could be refilled with cartridges much more quickly through the use of magazines. In the 1970s, police departments in the United States began slowly to replace revolvers with semiautomatic pistols. The replacement of revolvers by semiautomatic firearms is now a worldwide police trend. Yet many plainclothes police officers all over the world still use a remodeled type of revolver with a very short barrel that makes it easier to carry.

In Western-style democracies, the standard police sidearm is strictly a defensive weapon. For offensive operations such as gunfights, more powerful firearms—

for example, shotguns and rifles—are necessary. Shotguns are capable of firing a variety of ammunition, including buckshot, slugs, tear gas, baton projectiles, and grenades. The pump-action shotgun, which was widely used in police departments from the early twentieth century, began to be replaced by the semiautomatic shotgun in the late twentieth and early twenty-first centuries.

A police countersniper team gets into position before the start of Super Bowl XLVI in Indianapolis, Indiana, in 2012. Countersniper teams generally use high-precision rifles that have telescopic sights to enable magnification and the highest accuracy possible.

The lever-action rifle accompanied the lawmen of the American West as they policed their jurisdictions in the nineteenth century. During the twentieth century, police continued to use rifles of various descriptions and calibers. From the 1920s until World War II, some police departments in the United States adopted the Thompson submachine gun, or tommy gun, a weapon that was also embraced by the criminal underworld. The advent in the late 1960s of SWAT teams brought police countersniper units into service. Weapons used by such teams varied but typically included bolt-action high-caliber rifles fitted with telescopic sights.

EXPLOSIVES

Explosives are used only sparingly by police, generally for breaching barricades and as distraction devices. Explosive "flash-bangs," which generate a loud explosion and a brilliant flash that disorient suspects, are usually tossed by hand or launched from firearms. One variation of the flash-bang, used particularly for riot suppression, discharges multiple small rubber balls or baton projectiles. Other explosives can be used to deliver tear gas or aerosolized capsicum (pepper spray). Police also use sophisticated automated devices to handle explosives planted by terrorists or other criminals. Operated by police from a safe distance, the small tanklike vehicles with steel

A police bomb squad member and robot remove a suspicious device from a trash can in Portland, Maine. Police frequently use robots to retrieve and disarm explosive devices.

pincers can defuse or explode bombs after the public has been evacuated from the area.

SURVEILLANCE SYSTEMS

Audio surveillance, or electronic eavesdropping, became practical for obtaining evidence and investigating leads after the development of magnetic recording in the early twentieth century. Among the earliest automated surveillance systems were telephone pin registers, which recorded the phone numbers called from a certain surveillance location. Modern systems allow investigators to record the numbers of both incoming and outgoing calls, as well as any conversations. Other technologies enable audio surveillance through covert miniature microphones and radio transmitters and a variety of radio-receiving and voice-recording equipment. Self-contained wireless microphones are now so small that they can be hidden in virtually any object.

Police conduct visual surveillance with binoculars, telescopes, cameras with telephoto lenses, video recorders, and closed-circuit television (CCTV). Cameras fitted with telescopic and other specialty lenses have become a standard covert surveillance tool. Night-vision devices, or "starlight scopes," can be combined with telescopic lenses, both film and digital cameras, and video recorders. Similar to the forward-looking infrared units on aircraft, handheld passive thermal-imaging devices allow for covert observation in complete darkness. These instruments are particularly useful for searches inside unlit structures, for operations in which darkness must be maintained, and for locating lost persons in open areas.

CCTV is widely used by both public law enforcement and private security providers. Cameras may be equipped with telephoto or variable-power lenses and motor drives. Low-light cameras can record images in almost complete darkness; those equipped with

A police officer watches closed-circuit television (CCTV) monitors in London, England. CCTV cameras can be an important tool for surveillance in cities and are especially helpful in surveying huge public events and major disturbances.

infrared emitters can record images in total darkness. In high-risk operations, CCTV cameras enable police to look under doors, through windows, or around corners. They also may be placed in waterproof housings attached to cables as long as 150 feet (45 meters) to conduct underwater search operations. A specialized application of CCTV cameras captures images of drivers committing specific traffic offenses (such as speeding) and automatically issues citations to them. In addition, CCTV cameras are often placed in patrol vehicles to record traffic stops and other events. The recorded images may be used as evidence in court to confirm or refute allegations of improper or illegal conduct by police officers.

CCTV technology is used extensively in the United Kingdom to monitor both public and private spaces, including underground train stations, urban commercial spaces, suburban shopping malls, parking structures and loading bays, bus stations, supermarket aisles and entrances, hospital entrances and exits, workplaces, schools, police stations, and prisons. First implemented in the 1980s as a part of an initiative called Safer Cities, CCTV monitoring was eventually accepted by a majority of the British public despite initial objections from civil libertarians. Its popularity was boosted in 1993, when the taped abduction of a two-year-old boy helped to identify and convict those responsible for kidnapping and murdering him, and in 2005, when the system helped to identify the terrorists behind the bombings of London's public transportation system.

Some other countries, however, have opposed the use of CCTV in public spaces because they consider such monitoring by the police without prior grounds for suspicion to be an unacceptable infringement of civil liberties. Nevertheless, CCTV is used to monitor private spaces in nearly all countries, and its use in various public spaces continues to increase.

LIE DETECTORS

Throughout history, those responsible for enforcing the law have attempted to develop lie detectors. One ancient interrogation method used in Asia was based on the principle that salivation decreases during nervous tension. The mouths of several suspects were filled with dry rice, and the suspect exhibiting the greatest difficulty in spitting out the rice was judged guilty. In India, suspects were sent into a dark room where a sacred ass was stabled and were directed to pull the animal's tail. They were warned that if the ass brayed it was a sign of guilt. The ass's tail had been dusted with black powder; those with a clear conscience pulled the tail, whereas the guilty person did not, and an examination of the hands of the suspects revealed the person with the guilty conscience.

Scientific advances led to the development of polygraphs in the 1920s. The polygraph is based on the premise that an individual who is lying will have subtle but measurable changes in specific physical indicators. Lie detectors utilize sensors placed on the test subject to record respiration, heart rate, blood pressure, and galvanic skin response—a change in the flow of electrical current across the skin that can result from emotional arousal. Taken together under highly controlled interview conditions and interpreted by an

Detectives pose with a computer voice-stress analyzer (VSA) at a police department in Pennsylvania. VSAs measure changes in voice patterns that may indicate when a person is lying.

expert, the results of such measurements may indicate an attempt to deceive. Although the polygraph has proved an invaluable aid to police, its scientific validity has been questioned by some psychologists. Accordingly, the results of polygraph tests are not always admissible in court.

Voice-stress analyzers (VSAs), which became commercially available in the 1970s, rely on the detection of minute variations in the voice of the subject. Advocates of voice-stress analysis contend that inaudible vibrations in the voice, known as microtremors, speed up when a person is lying. During a VSA test, computer equipment measures the microtremors in a subject's voice and displays their patterns on a screen; certain patterns may indicate lies. Despite their initial promise, VSAs have not gained universal acceptance; critics argue that VSAs cannot distinguish between stress that results from lying and high stress in general. Other lie-detection techniques developed in the late twentieth century relied on thermal images of facial-skin temperature and on measurements of brain-wave activity.

CHAPTER THREE

CRIMINAL IDENTIFICATION

Criminal identification based on various scientific methods has acquired a mythical dimension thanks to popular fictional accounts of police investigation. However, scientific methods of criminal identification are actually more useful for producing evidence to be used in court to secure the conviction of a suspect—typically identified through the traditional investigative method of questioning the witnesses of a crime—than they are for identifying who the perpetrator of a crime is, particularly if the perpetrator has no previous criminal record.

Scientific means of criminal identification can be classified in two categories. The oldest and most traditional means, such as photography and anthropometry, depend initially on the arrest of a suspect, who is then photographed and described physically. These photographs and anthropometric descriptions can be used at a future time to reidentify a criminal, but this person needs to have been caught in a first offense to trigger the system. Newer identification techniques have no such limitations. They do not consist of depictions of a whole individual; rather, they involve the scientific analysis of traces that a perpetrator may leave behind—for example, fingerprints or blood (a source of DNA). The results of such analyses can be matched with the physical characteristics of a suspect who has never been arrested before and thus can result in a new positive identification.

Nevertheless, the few studies of criminal investigation that have been conducted stress the limited contribution of such scientific methods to the identification of unknown perpetrators. The most efficient identification technique—that is, the questioning of witnesses—is also the most time-honored. The probability of solving a crime drops dramatically when there are no witnesses of any kind.

PHOTOGRAPHY

As early as the 1840s in Brussels, Belgium, police used photographs to keep track of criminals. Such

An FBI agent (*left*) places "in custody" stickers on a poster that shows the mug shots of seventy-five gang members and their associates who have been arrested during raids in Los Angeles, California. Officers use mug shots to help them identify repeat offenders whose photographs are already on file.

photographs, or mug shots, are an essential tool for police investigators. A variety of different formats have been used—including, most recently, digital images—and there is no single universal system employed throughout the world. Digital mug shots have the advantage of being instantly transmittable anywhere in the world via the internet.

ANTHROPOMETRY

The science of anthropometry was developed in the late nineteenth century by Alphonse Bertillon, chief of criminal identification for the Paris police. The Bertillon system, which gained almost immediate acceptance worldwide, used meticulous physical measurements of body parts, especially the head and face, to produce a detailed description, or *portrait parlé.* Initially, the system was used much less to identify unknown perpetrators than to allow investigators to determine whether the suspects they arrested had been involved in previous crimes. Known recidivists (repeat offenders) were believed to be more dangerous and were accordingly punished more severely.

FINGERPRINTING

Anthropometry was largely supplanted by modern fingerprinting, which developed during roughly the same period, though the origins of fingerprinting date from thousands of years ago. As noted previously in the introduction, the Babylonians pressed fingerprints into clay to identify the author of cuneiform writings and to protect against forgery. The Chinese also were using fingerprints in about 800 CE for purposes of identification.

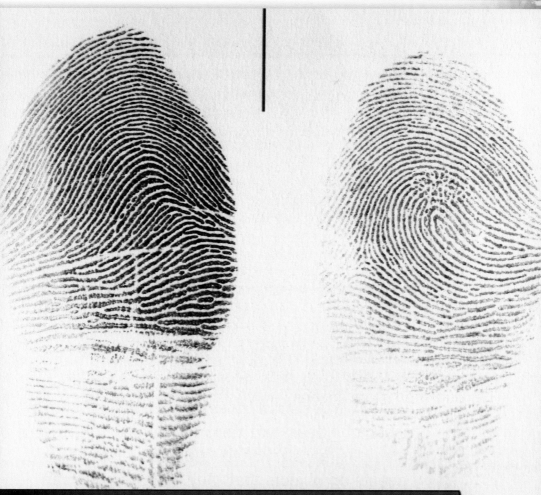

Fingerprints display the patterns made by the ridges on the ends of fingers and thumbs. Fingerprints are a very reliable means of personal identification because the ridge arrangement on every finger of every person is unique and does not alter with growth or age.

Following the pioneering work of Francis Galton, Britain adopted fingerprinting as a form of identification in 1894. In Argentina, police officer Juan Vucetich, inspired by Galton's work, developed the first workable system of classifying fingerprints—a system still widely used in many Spanish-speaking countries. In Britain, a system of classifying prints by patterns and shapes based on Galton's work and further developed by Sir Edward R. Henry was accepted by Scotland Yard in 1901. That system, or variants of it, soon became the standard fingerprint-classification method throughout the English-speaking world.

Fingerprint identification, or the science of dactyloscopy, relies on the analysis and classification of patterns observed in individual prints. Fingerprints are made of series of ridges and furrows on the surface of a finger; the loops, whorls, and arches formed by those ridges and furrows generally follow a number of distinct patterns. Fingerprints also contain individual characteristics called "minutiae," such as the number of ridges and their groupings, that are not perceptible to the naked eye. The fingerprints left by people on objects that they have touched can be either visible or latent. Visible prints may be left behind by substances that stick to the fingers—such as dirt or blood—or they may take the form of an impression made in a soft substance, such as clay. Latent fingerprints are traces of sweat, oil, or other natural secretions on the skin, and they are not ordinarily visible. Latent fingerprints can be made visible by dusting techniques when the surface is hard and by chemical techniques when the surface is porous.

Fingerprints provide police with extremely strong physical evidence tying suspects to evidence or crime scenes. Yet, until the computerization of fingerprint records, there was no practical way of identifying a suspect solely on the basis of latent fingerprints left at a crime scene, because police would not know which set of prints on file (if any) might match those left by the suspect. This changed in the 1980s when the Japanese National Police Agency established the first practical system for matching prints electronically. Today, police in most countries use such systems, called automated fingerprint identification systems (AFIS), to search rapidly through millions of digitized fingerprint records. Fingerprints recognized by AFIS are examined by a fingerprint analyst before a positive identification or match is made.

DNA FINGERPRINTING

The technique of DNA fingerprinting, which involves comparing samples of human DNA left at a crime scene with DNA obtained from a suspect, is now considered the most reliable form of identification by many investigators and scientists. Since its development in the 1980s, DNA fingerprinting has led to the conviction of numerous criminals and to the freeing from prison of many individuals who were wrongly convicted.

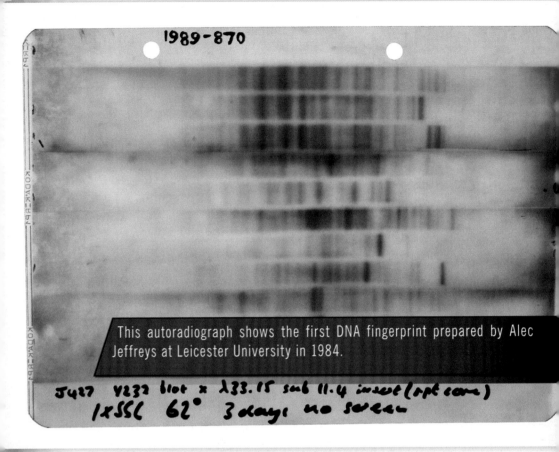

1989-870

This autoradiograph shows the first DNA fingerprint prepared by Alec Jeffreys at Leicester University in 1984.

The Combined DNA Index System (CODIS), developed by the US Department of Justice and the FBI, combines computer technology with forensics, enabling investigators to compare DNA samples against a database of DNA records of convicted offenders and others. CODIS is used worldwide for sharing and comparing DNA data; it is available for free to all police forensics laboratories. The first national DNA fingerprinting database (NDNAD) in the United Kingdom was established

GETTING A DNA FINGERPRINT

DNA fingerprinting involves isolating and identifying variable elements within the base-pair sequence of DNA. The
technique was developed in 1984 by British geneticist Alec
Jeffreys, after he noticed that certain sequences of highly
variable DNA (known as minisatellites), which do not con-
tribute to the functions of genes, are repeated within genes.
Jeffreys recognized that each individual has a unique pattern
of minisatellites (the only exceptions being multiple individuals from a single zygote, such as identical twins).

The procedure for creating a DNA fingerprint consists of
first obtaining a sample of cells, such as skin, hair, or blood
cells, which contain DNA. The DNA is extracted from the
cells and purified. In Jeffreys's original approach, which was
based on restriction fragment length polymorphism (RFLP)
technology, the DNA was then cut at specific points along
the strand with proteins known as restriction enzymes. The
enzymes produced fragments of varying lengths that were
sorted by placing them on a gel and then subjecting the gel
to an electric current: the shorter the fragment, the more
quickly it moved toward the positive pole (anode). The
sorted double-stranded DNA fragments were then subjected
to a blotting technique in which they were split into single strands and transferred to a nylon sheet. The fragments
underwent autoradiography in which they were exposed
to DNA probes—pieces of synthetic DNA that were made

(continued on the next page)

(continued from the previous page)

radioactive and that bound to the minisatellites. A piece of X-ray film was then exposed to the fragments, and a dark mark was produced at any point where a radioactive probe had become attached. The resultant pattern of marks could then be analyzed.

The process developed by Jeffreys has been supplanted by approaches that are based on the use of the polymerase chain reaction (PCR) and so-called microsatellites (or short tandem repeats, STRs), which have shorter repeat units (typically two to four base pairs in length) than minisatellites (ten to more than a hundred base pairs in length). PCR amplifies the desired fragment of DNA (for example, a specific STR) many times over, creating thousands of copies of the fragment. It is an automated procedure that requires only small amounts of DNA as starting material and works even with partially degraded DNA. Once an adequate amount of DNA has been produced with PCR, the exact sequence of nucleotide pairs in a segment of DNA can be determined by using one of several biomolecular sequencing methods. Automated equipment has greatly increased the speed of DNA sequencing and has made available many new practical applications, including pinpointing segments of genes that cause genetic diseases, mapping the human genome, engineering drought-resistant plants, and producing biological drugs from genetically altered bacteria.

An early use of DNA fingerprinting was in legal disputes, notably to help solve crimes and to determine paternity. The technique was challenged, however, over concerns about sample contamination, faulty preparation procedures, and erroneous interpretation of the results. In addition, RFLP required large amounts of high-quality DNA, which limited its application in forensics. Forensic DNA samples frequently are degraded or are collected postmortem, which means that they are lower-quality and subject to producing less-reliable results than samples that are obtained from a living individual. Some of the concerns with DNA fingerprinting, and specifically the use of RFLP, subsided with the development of PCR- and STR-based approaches.

in 1995. Other countries, including France, Canada, and Japan, created DNA databases as well.

Although DNA fingerprinting cannot empirically produce a perfect positive identification, the probability of error—a false positive—can be decreased to a point that it seems nonexistent. When enough tests are performed, and when the DNA sample is suitable, DNA testing can show that a suspect cannot be excluded as the source of the sample. Sufficient testing also may exclude virtually every other individual in the world as the source of the sample. However, making scientific identification coincide exactly with legal proof will always remain problematic. As low as it may be, even a single suggestion of the possibility of error is sometimes enough to persuade a jury not to convict a suspect, as was shown spectacularly by the acquittal of O. J. Simpson, the American former football star, of murder charges in 1995. By contrast, DNA can clear a suspect of guilt with absolute certainty. If there is no DNA match between a sample taken from a crime scene and a sample provided by a suspect, then there is no possibility at all that the DNA-fingerprinted suspect may be guilty. Consequently, DNA fingerprinting is playing a crucial role in proving the innocence of persons wrongly convicted of violent crimes.

BIOMETRICS

In criminal investigations, biometric analysis, or biometrics, can be used to identify suspects by means of various unique biological markers. Biometric devices can map minutiae in a single fingerprint and then compare it with an exemplar on file, conduct a retinal or iris scan of the eye, measure and map an entire handprint, or create a digital map of the face.

Biometric facial-mapping systems, or "facecams," when linked to offender databases and CCTV cameras in public places, can be used to identify offenders and alert police. Such facecam systems were implemented

The airport in Frankfurt, Germany, has a border-control system that uses biometrics. A passenger with an electronic passport places the document on a scanner. Then a camera takes a picture of the passenger to compare to the passport photo. If the biometric data matches and the passenger is not on a watch list, the border gate opens.

in London and other areas of Britain beginning in the 1990s and in several US cities and airports in the early twenty-first century. Some advocates of biometric technology have proposed that biometric data be embedded into driver's licenses or passports to enable security officials to identify suspects quickly; such arguments were made more frequently after the September 11 attacks in 2001. However, critics of the technology contend that it unduly infringes upon the civil liberties of law-abiding citizens; they also point out that biometric systems such as facecams and thumbprint matching would not have identified most of the hijackers involved in the September 11 attacks—much less foiled their plot—because only two of the nineteen hijackers were on the CIA's "watch list."

CHAPTER FOUR

CRIME-SCENE INVESTIGATION AND FORENSIC SCIENCES

T he first police crime laboratory was established in 1910 in Lyon, France, by Edmond Locard. According to Locard's "exchange principle," it is impossible for criminals to escape a crime scene without leaving behind trace evidence that can be used to identify them. That principle gave rise to the forensic sciences, which are methods for developing and analyzing physical evidence from crime scenes. Crime-scene investigation, which is often performed by experts known as crime-scene investigators (CSIs), involves the careful gathering of such evidence, which is then analyzed at a crime laboratory. In some cases, evidence gathered by CSIs and analyzed by forensic experts is the only incontrovertible evidence presented at trial.

A crime-scene investigator (CSI) from a California police department examines a gun that was used in a shooting. Police have to be meticulous when collecting evidence at a crime scene.

EVIDENCE COLLECTION

Because there is rarely more than one opportunity to obtain evidence from a crime scene, the investigation by the CSIs must be methodical and complete. In keeping with Locard's exchange principle, CSIs collect evidence from the crime scene that may have been touched or microscopically "contaminated" by the suspect or suspects. They also take samples of fibers, dirt, and dust.

After a preliminary search, the crime scene is photographed; some police departments also make a videotape of the scene. CSIs take careful measurements, make detailed notes, and draw sketches. Evidence is collected and carefully catalogued. Scientific and technological advances have resulted in the development of laser and alternative-light sources that can reveal latent fingerprints, stains, hairs, fibers, and other trace evidence. For example, luminol, a substance that fluoresces (glows) when in contact with blood, is capable of detecting blood traces that have been diluted up to 10,000 times, making it useful for searching crime scenes that were cleaned

At a trial in New Zealand, a forensics expert shows a picture of a suspect's bloody footprint that was treated with luminol. Before spraying luminol at a crime scene, there often is no indication of blood. However, after luminol is used, blood traces give off a bluish glow.

to conceal evidence. In addition, the patterns of blood stains often indicate many of the dynamics of the crime; investigators trained in blood-pattern analysis, for example, can determine whether a victim was standing still, walking, or running at the time of death. Although some larger police departments have specialists to take photographs and fingerprints and to collect trace evidence, most CSIs are generalists who are trained to perform all these tasks.

FORENSIC ANALYSIS

Forensic science plays an important role in the investigation of serious crimes. It has many branches because different types of evidence require different methods of forensic analysis. Forensics specialists investigate microscopic fibers such as hair as well as blood and other human fluids. Some forensic examiners study handwriting and help authenticate documents. Others specialize in ballistics.

HAIRS AND FIBERS

Although a single hair or fiber cannot place a suspect at a crime scene, collections of hair or fiber can be used to establish with a high degree of probability that the suspect is connected to the crime. Hairs possess class

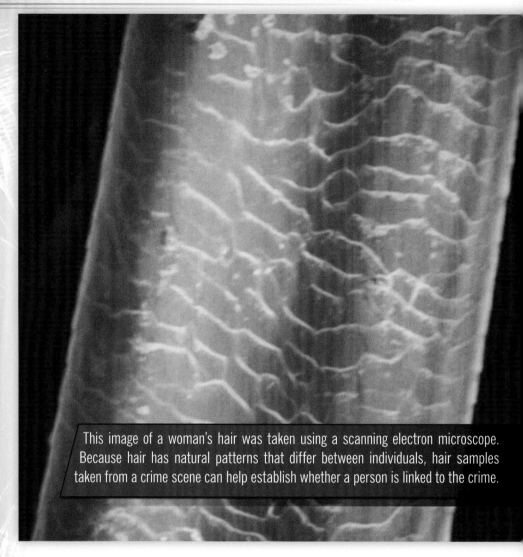

This image of a woman's hair was taken using a scanning electron microscope. Because hair has natural patterns that differ between individuals, hair samples taken from a crime scene can help establish whether a person is linked to the crime.

characteristics (patterns that naturally occur in specific percentages of the population) that indicate some general features of the individual from whom they are obtained, such as what diseases he may have and sometimes what race he belongs to. If the hair has any follicular material or blood on it, a DNA test can determine with a certain

CRIME LABORATORY

A crime laboratory is a facility where analyses are performed on evidence generated by crimes or, sometimes, civil infractions. Crime laboratories can investigate physical, chemical, biological, or digital evidence and often employ specialists in a variety of disciplines, including behavioral forensic science, forensic pathology, forensic anthropology, crime-scene investigation, and ballistics. Many crime labs are publicly funded and administered by federal, state or provincial, or local government, although there are a growing number of private labs that specialize in fields such as drug analysis and DNA fingerprinting. England and Wales are among the few places in the world to have exclusively privatized crime labs.

Of the approximately four hundred public crime labs in the United States, only a handful are administered by the federal government. One of the most famous of those is that of the Federal Bureau of Investigation (FBI), which processes evidence from FBI investigations and from violent crimes submitted by US law-enforcement agencies, free of cost. At the state level, all states maintain a crime-lab system, though there have been limited efforts at coordination and regional planning between states. Many city and county labs are independent of statewide systems. The majority of labs are located within police or sheriff's departments, although some are run by prosecutors or the state department of justice.

(continued on the next page)

(continued from the previous page)

A few have been subsumed within medical examiner's labs, and some are associated with universities.

All crime labs have some sort of evidence-intake unit, where evidence is received and assigned a unique laboratory and case identifier. That may be a number assigned by a clerk or a bar code affixed to each item and tracked by computer. The bar-code system generates an automatic chain of custody of the evidence and makes it possible to determine its location in the lab at any time.

From log-in, the evidence is usually stored in a secure environment, which may be a temporary storage area or the main storage area for all evidence in the lab, until it is assigned to one or more examiners. Examiners may have separate storage areas for their own evidence. From here, crime labs vary greatly and offer different levels of service. In a system of regional laboratories, there is generally at least one lab that offers all the services available in that state or province, whereas others offer less-comprehensive services.

degree of probability whether the sample came from a particular individual.

TOXICOLOGY

Toxicology was first systematized in the nineteenth century by the Spanish physician Matthieu Orfila.

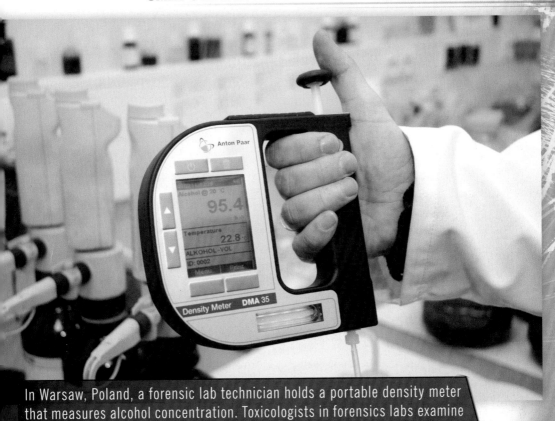

In Warsaw, Poland, a forensic lab technician holds a portable density meter that measures alcohol concentration. Toxicologists in forensics labs examine human blood and other body fluids for the presence of alcohol or drugs.

Toxicologists examine blood and tissues to ascertain the presence and quantity of drugs or poisons in a person's body. Toxicological reports can assist investigators by showing whether the drug ingested was fatal and the approximate time the drug was introduced into the body.

The toxicology unit of a crime lab often supports the work of the medical examiner and may be located within that office. Forensic toxicologists are also responsible for determining the alcohol concentration in blood in drunk-driving cases and may provide training and maintenance of field alcohol-testing instruments.

SEROLOGY

Serology is the study of serums such as blood and other human fluids. In 1901, Karl Landsteiner, a researcher at the University of Vienna, published his discovery that human blood could be grouped into distinct types, which became known as the ABO blood group system. In 1915, the Italian scientist Leone Lattes developed a simple method for determining the blood type of a dried bloodstain. The Rh blood group system, which classifies blood according to the presence or absence of the Rh antigen, was developed in 1939–1940. Since that time, more than one hundred different blood factors have been discovered. Because those factors appear unevenly in the population, they can be used to identify the particular groups to which potential suspects belong. As various blood factors are defined in a sample, the percentage of people who have that combination of factors is narrowed, and the sample becomes more individualized. The introduction into forensics of DNA analysis has enabled investigators to detect identifying characteristics of body fluids and cells with unprecedented precision, making them better able to implicate or eliminate potential suspects.

EXAMINING DOCUMENTS

The work of the "questioned document" examiner concerns such problems as identifying handwriting and typewriting, determining the age of a document, and determining the sequence of events involved in a document's preparation, handling, or alteration. Document examiners employ a variety of technologies and techniques. Handwriting analysis, for example, is based on the premise that, by the time people become adults, their writing has acquired peculiarities that may be used to identify them.

A forged signature presents other problems. Simulated signatures based upon recollection contain a combination of the forger's own writing habits and his recollection of the victim's habits. In many cases, such simulations can be identified. When the perpetrator makes a careful drawing of the victim's signature or traces an authentic signature, however, the forgery can be exposed but cannot be identified with the handwriting of the perpetrator. Two individuals making careful tracings of the same signature can produce virtually identical drawings.

In the era before computers, investigators would sometimes examine typewriters to determine the make and model used to prepare a document. Ink comparisons provided evidence that was frequently

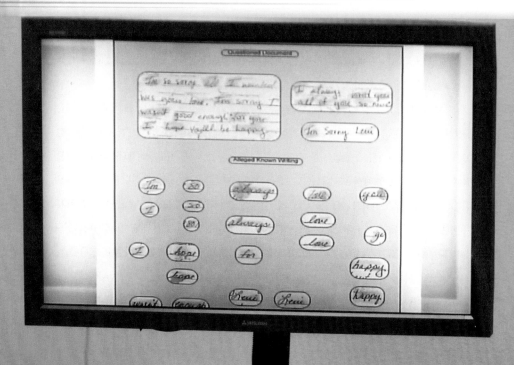

A handwriting expert testifies about two notes during a murder trial in New Mexico.

of value. Chemical tests of various kinds are used for ink comparisons.

Papers can be differentiated on the basis of fiber, filler, and sizing constituents. Fibers can be identified by differential staining and microscopic examination. Fillers can be distinguished by X-ray diffraction because they are crystalline substances. Chemical tests are used for the identification of sizing constituents. Through chemical analysis, it is even possible to identify paper by batches.

FIREARMS AND TOOL MARKS

Firearms identification was developed in the 1920s by American ballistics expert Calvin Goddard, who first applied his new technique to help solve the St. Valentine's Day Massacre in Chicago, Illinois, in 1929. Each firearm leaves individual markings on a bullet and case when it is fired. Such markings can be used to determine whether evidentiary bullets were fired from a suspect weapon. Similar techniques are applied to marks left behind at crime scenes by pry bars, screwdrivers, wire cutters, and other tools.

Analyses in the firearms and tool-marks unit of a crime lab include comparison of spent bullets and cartridges to weapons, determination of distance of firing, ability of a weapon to fire, and restoration of obliterated

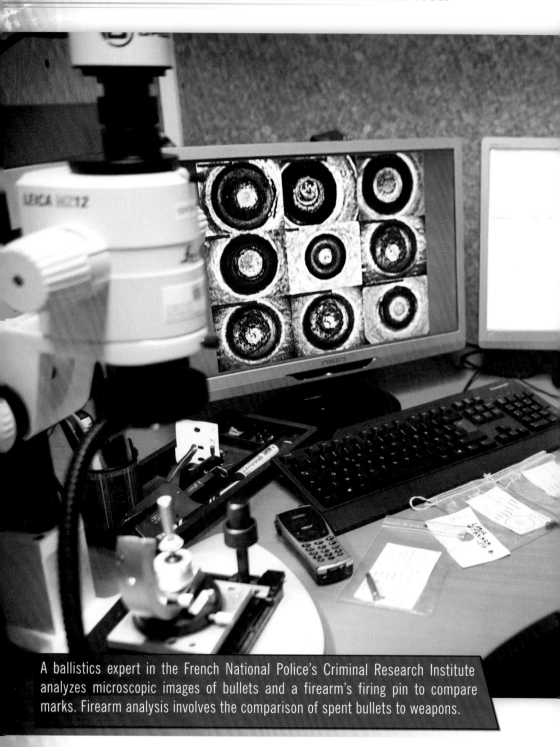

A ballistics expert in the French National Police's Criminal Research Institute analyzes microscopic images of bullets and a firearm's firing pin to compare marks. Firearm analysis involves the comparison of spent bullets to weapons.

serial numbers on weapons. In a number of countries, markings on a shell or bullet are photographed through a microscope and compared with information in national databases.

ORGANIC AND INORGANIC ANALYSIS

Police use organic and inorganic analysis to examine the chemical composition of trace evidence found at a crime scene, which may then be matched to substances associated with a suspect. Organic analysis, which is performed on substances containing carbon atoms, involves various techniques, including chromatography, spectrophotometry, and mass spectrometry. Inorganic analysis, which is performed on all substances that do not contain carbon, employs spectrophotometry, neutron-activation analysis (a technique involving chemical analysis by radioactivity), and X-ray diffraction, among other techniques.

SUPPLEMENTAL FORENSIC SCIENCES

Various other life and physical sciences are used to assist police investigations. Specialists approach the problem from different scientific perspectives, and the results of their investigations can provide police with a wealth of information about a case.

Forensic pathology is a specialty within the field of medical pathology. Forensic pathologists conduct an

Forensic anthropologists examine human bones to identify the person from whom they came.

autopsy in cases of violent, unexplained, or unattended deaths, closely examining the decedent's wounds, blood, and tissue to ascertain how he or she died. Often said to be "speaking for the dead," forensic pathologists can establish a cause and a rough time of death and can often provide clues regarding the physical characteristics of the person or persons responsible for the crime.

Forensic anthropology is primarily concerned with the identification of human skeletal remains. Forensic anthropologists can differentiate animal remains from those of humans and, given the proper bones, can determine the gender and in some cases the race of the victim. In the 1970s, American forensic anthropologist William Bass established the first human-decay research facility, known as the "body farm," at the University of Tennessee, Knoxville. The center's studies of the physical changes that decomposing corpses undergo over time have helped to establish an empirical basis for estimating time of death.

Facial reconstruction combines both art and science. A skull can be used as a foundation and the face reconstructed with clay. By using charts of specific points of skin and tissue thickness, scientists can produce a relatively unique face that can then be used to help identify the decedent.

Forensic entomology is another field that assists police in determining time of death. Insects infest a corpse at a very predictable rate. Certain insects immediately invade the body to feed or to lay eggs, while

FORENSIC ANTHROPOLOGISTS AND FORENSIC INVESTIGATION

Forensic anthropologists may work with bodies in a variety of conditions, including as mummies, piles of bones, decomposed bodies, charred remains, and the victims of aircraft crashes or natural catastrophes. Investigations often begin with a ground search team using cadaver dogs or a low-flying plane to locate a missing body or skeleton. As a meticulous examination of any death scene is imperative, forensic anthropologists are frequently involved at the earliest stages of investigating a human skeleton. After mapping, photographing, and labeling relevant items at the scene, the bone evidence is examined at a forensic laboratory. Bone fragments are sorted according to size and shape and fitted together when possible.

Forensic anthropologists focus on human skeletal traits, such as skull features and dental characteristics, that vary from individual to individual and from population to population. When compared with medical and dental records, the presence of bone anomalies, metal plates or pins, or specific dental characteristics can help to make a positive identification. In addition to revealing the age, sex, size, stature, health, and ethnic population of the decedent, an examination of the skeleton may reveal evidence concerning pathology and any antemortem (before death), perimortem (at the time of death), or postmortem (after death) trauma. Often the time elapsed since death can be determined by using forensic entomology, which studies the relationship between insects and decomposition.

The adult human skeleton has 206 bones, although this number may vary among individuals; a person may have an extra vertebra or rib. Generally, the adult male skeleton is larger and more robust in appearance than the adult female skeleton. The general age of an individual may be determined by skull size, condition of sutures, and an examination of the teeth, as well as by the length of particular bones (for example, the femur and the humerus) and the degree of ossification (bone hardening) that has taken place between the shaft of a long bone and its end caps.

In the case of victims with gunshot wounds to the head, a forensic study of bullet holes and fractures in a skull can determine the trajectory of bullets through the cranium. An entrance wound is generally smaller and rounder, whereas the usually larger exit wound is more ragged and shows external beveling. Markings on a shell or bullet are photographed through a microscope and compared with information in a national database for definite identification. If a bullet is not found, then X-rays of the skull may reveal bullet fragments.

others will not approach the body until it has reached a more advanced stage of decomposition. Thus, the types of insects or eggs present in a corpse indicate how long the victim has been dead. A forensic entomologist can

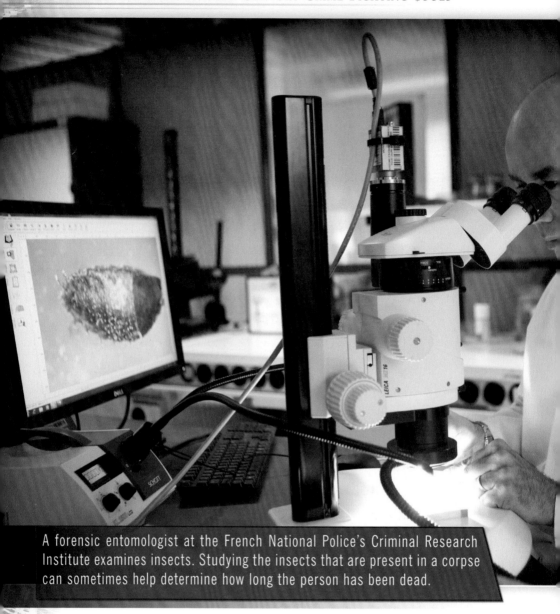

A forensic entomologist at the French National Police's Criminal Research Institute examines insects. Studying the insects that are present in a corpse can sometimes help determine how long the person has been dead.

also assist in determining where packages or cargo originated if insects or eggs are found in the shipment.

Forensic odontologists examine teeth and bite marks. They can compare the teeth of an unidentified

body with an individual's antemortem dental X-rays or dental molds. They also may tie a suspect to a crime by comparing a bite mark taken from the crime scene with dental casts taken from the suspect.

Forensic botanists examine plants and plant matter to determine their species and origin. In some cases, suspects may leave behind plant parts, spores, or seeds that had adhered to their clothing. If the plant species in question is found only in limited areas, its presence at the crime scene may indicate where suspects have been or where they live. Forensic botanists can also be essential in locating clandestine gardens or greenhouses used to cultivate such illegal plants as marijuana.

Forensic engineers perform accident reconstructions and failure analyses of vehicles and structures. The science of forensic engineering was instrumental in understanding the physical dynamics of the Oklahoma City bombing in 1995 and in explaining the collapse of the twin towers of the World Trade Center in the September 11 attacks of 2001. Forensic engineering is also useful in police investigations of motor-vehicle accidents.

A forensic engineer and a police officer work through the wreckage of a car after a bomb blast in Berlin, Germany. Forensic engineers analyze the debris after an accident or explosion to determine how the incident occurred.

Forensic art or illustration is used for reconstructing crime or accident scenes. Artists can produce sketches of suspects from the recollections of victims or witnesses; they can also produce illustrations to assist prosecutors in court. An increasingly used technique involves illustrating the step-by-step development of accidents or crimes by means of computer-generated animations.

As the use of computers and the internet in all types of activities grew rapidly in the late twentieth and early

James Comey, director of the US Federal Bureau of Investigation (FBI), appears before the House Judiciary Committee in 2016. In the aftermath of the December 2015 terrorist attack in San Bernardino, California, the FBI wanted a phone manufacturer to be forced to unlock the encrypted device used by one of the shooters.

twenty-first centuries, forensic computing became an important field for investigating cybercrimes, including crimes involving computer hacking (the illegal entry into and use of a computer network) and the programming and distribution of malicious computer viruses. In many cases, personal computers are confiscated at crime scenes or pursuant to warrants. Police may require the assistance of a computer expert to break any password protections or to unlock encrypted files to reveal evidence of criminal activity.

CONCLUSION

The ways in which police organizations enforce laws, identify and apprehend suspects, examine criminal evidence, and work to reduce crime have changed dramatically during the last fifty years. Remarkable new progress has been made. Most of the advances have resulted from technological discoveries and inventions in many areas: transportation,

A patrol officer in West Valley City, Utah, wears a body camera that is attached to a pair of eyeglasses. The city issued body cameras to all its police so that interactions with the public could be recorded.

communication, computer science, weaponry, surveillance, DNA fingerprinting, forensic analysis, and others.

The "smoking gun" of yesteryear was considered clear evidence that the bearer of the firearm was the person who recently fired it. Frequently today, "smoking guns" that help prove criminals' guilt are not pistols, rifles, or shotguns. More likely, they are hard-to-detect traces of paint, strands of hair, threads of clothing, bits of clay, dental X-rays, barely visible skin markings, and traces of poison. From these and other particles of microscopic evidence, scientists and technical specialists can read strange but true tales of violence and deception and accurately interpret the role each one played in a criminal mystery.

Twenty-first-century criminals are using the internet and many other technological innovations to perpetrate malice of every type. Police organizations are adapting technology to keep up with the miscreants and, hopefully, stay one step ahead of them.

1829 The Metropolitan Police Act is passed in England, establishing the London Metropolitan Police Department.

1840s Police in Brussels, Belgium, use photographs to keep track of criminals.

1870s Police departments install telephone systems for communication.

1882 The Bertillon system of criminal identification is introduced.

1894 Great Britain adopts fingerprinting as a form of identification.

1901 Karl Landsteiner discovers that human blood can be grouped into distinct types.

1910 The first crime lab is set up in Lyon, France.

1911 John Browning patents the .45-caliber single-action semiautomatic pistol.

1917 New York City equips patrol vehicles with one-way radios to enable the central command to send emergency messages to officers.

1920s Polygraphs are developed.

1928 The police department of Detroit, Michigan, achieves regular radio contact between police headquarters and patrol units.

1933 Bayonne, New Jersey, deploys the first two-way radio receivers.

1937 London establishes the first emergency telephone system.

1960s Bulletproof vests are developed from steel or boron carbide. The 911 emergency telephone system is instituted in the United States.

1967 The United States establishes the National Crime Information Center.

1970s The electronic device TASER is introduced as a nonlethal weapon for police. US police departments begin to replace revolvers with semiautomatic pistols.

1980s Great Britain uses CCTV as part of Safer Cities initiative. Japan's National Police Agency establishes the first system for matching fingerprints electronically. DNA fingerprinting is developed.

1985 The Schengen Agreement is approved by Belgium, France, West Germany (later Germany), Luxembourg, and the Netherlands to begin reducing internal border controls. It creates the Schengen Information System for sharing information about people and goods traveling in the Schengen zone.

1990s The PepperBall, a nonlethal device, is first used by members of law enforcement. Facecam systems are implemented in Great Britain.

1995 The first national DNA fingerprinting database is created in the United Kingdom.

2012 The Middle Class Tax Relief and Job Creation Act is signed into law, creating the First Responder Network Authority (FirstNet).

GLOSSARY

ALLEGATION A statement not supported by definite proof or evidence.

ANTHROPOMETRY The study of the human body through measurement to determine physical patterns.

BALLISTICS The study of the firing of projectiles (such as bullets), their flight, and how they strike a target.

BIOMETRICS The measurement and analysis of unique physical or behavioral characteristics (such as fingerprint or voice patterns), especially as a means of verifying personal identity.

BLACKJACK A small leather-covered club with a flexible handle.

BREATHALYZER A device that determines the alcohol content of a breath sample, which is directly related to the alcohol content of the blood.

BRIGADE A group of people organized to act together.

CHROMATOGRAPHY A process for separating the components, or solutes, of a mixture on the basis of the relative amounts of each solute as they flow around or over a stationary liquid or solid phase.

CITATION An official order to appear before a court of law.

CIVIL LIBERTARIAN One who upholds the principles of civil liberty—freedom from arbitrary interference in one's pursuits by individuals or by government.

COVERT Secret or hidden.

DACTYLOSCOPY Identification by comparison of fingerprints; also the classification of fingerprints.

DEFIBRILLATOR A device that administers electric shocks to the heart to reset normal heart rhythm in someone who is experiencing cardiac arrest.

DISPATCH To send quickly to a particular place for a particular purpose.

MASS SPECTROMETRY An instrumental method for identifying the chemical constitution of a substance by means of the separation of gaseous ions according to their differing mass and charge.

MISCREANT A criminal.

MISDEMEANOR A crime less serious than a felony.

NONLETHAL Not causing death.

PERPETRATOR One who is guilty of a crime or offense.

POSTMORTEM Done or occurring after death.

SPECTROPHOTOMETRY The process of measuring the relative intensities of the light in the different parts of a spectrum.

SURREPTITIOUSLY Secretly done, made, or acquired.

WARRANT A legal paper giving an officer the power to make an arrest, a seizure, or a search or to do other acts necessary to carry out the law.

X-RAY DIFFRACTION A method of analyzing the crystal structure of materials by passing X-rays through them and observing the diffraction, or scattering, image of the rays.

FOR MORE INFORMATION

American Polygraph Association (APA)
PO Box 8037
Chattanooga, TN 37414-0037
(800) 272-8037
Website: http://www.polygraph.org
> The APA represents more than 2,800 polygraph examiners in private industry, law enforcement, and government. It creates standards of ethical practices and methods and offers advanced training and education programs.

American Society of Criminology (ASC)
1314 Kinnear Road, Suite 212
Columbus, OH 43212-1156
(614) 292-9207
Website: https:www.asc41.com
> The ASC encourages scholarly, scientific, and professional knowledge regarding the measurement, causes, consequences, and prevention of crime worldwide.

Bureau of Alcohol, Tobacco, Firearms and Explosives (ATF)
Science and Technology
99 New York Avenue NE
Washington, DC 20226
(202) 648-8390
Website: https://www.atf.gov

The ATF is an organization within the US Department of Justice. It works to combat the illegal use and trafficking of firearms, the illegal use of explosives, acts of arson and bombings, acts of terrorism, and the illegal diversion of alcohol and tobacco products.

Canadian Society of Forensic Science
PO Box 37040
3332 McCarthy Road
Ottawa, ON K1V 0W0
Canada
(613) 738-0001
Website: http://csfs.ca
This professional organization promotes the study of forensic science in Canada.

Federal Bureau of Investigation (FBI)
FBI Headquarters
935 Pennsylvania Avenue NW
Washington, DC 20535-0001
(202) 324-3000
Website: https://www.fbi.gov
The FBI investigates numerous crimes and national security concerns, including those involving terrorism, counterintelligence, cybercrimes, weapons of mass destruction, public corruption, civil rights, organized crime, white-collar crime,

and violent crime and major thefts. Its laboratory in Virginia employs about five hundred scientists and special agents.

International Association of Crime Analysts (IACA)
9218 Metcalf Avenue #364
Overland Park, KS 66212
(800) 609-3419
Website: http://www.iaca.net
    Established in 1990, the IACA assists crime analysts worldwide in improving their skills and connecting with other professionals in the field.

Law Enforcement Cyber Center (LECC)
44 Canal Center Plaza, Suite 200
Alexandria, VA 22314
(703) 836-6767 or (800) THE-IACP
Website: http://www.iacpcybercenter.org
This center helps police chiefs, patrol officers, digital forensic investigators, detectives, and prosecutors who work to prevent crimes that involve technology.

Royal Canadian Mounted Police (RCMP)
Headquarters Building
73 Leikin Drive
Ottawa, ON K1A 0R2
Canada
(613) 993-7267

Website: http://www.rcmp-grc.gc.ca
> The RCMP is Canada's national police force. Its mission includes enforcing laws, investigating and preventing crime, maintaining peace and order, and safeguarding national security.

US Department of Homeland Security
Website: http://www.dhs.gov
> The Department of Homeland Security aims to protect the United States from various threats. Its mission includes securing and managing US borders and administering immigration laws, preventing terrorism and enhancing security, preventing cyber-attacks, and responding to natural disasters or other large-scale emergencies. See https://www.dhs.gov/direct-contact-information to find contact information for the department's various divisions.

WEBSITES

Because of the changing nature of internet links, Rosen Publishing has developed an online list of websites related to the subject of this book. This site is updated regularly. Please use this link to access the list:

http://www.rosenlinks.com/BLAW/ptech

FOR FURTHER READING

Brezina, Corona. *Careers in the Homicide Unit* (Extreme Law Enforcement). New York, NY: Rosen Publishing, 2014.

Britz, Marjie T. *Computer Forensics and Cyber Crime: An Introduction*. 3d ed. Boston, MA: Pearson, 2013.

Curley, Rob, ed. *Spy Agencies, Intelligence Operations, and the People Behind Them* (Intelligence and Counterintelligence). New York, NY: Britannica Educational Publishing and Rosen Educational Services, 2014.

Dempsey, John S., and Linda S. Forst. *Police*. Clifton Park, NY: Delmar Cengage Learning, 2013.

Grinapol, Corinne. *Careers on Antiterrorism & Counterterrorism Task Forces* (Extreme Law Enforcement). New York, NY: Rosen Publishing, 2014.

Hunter, William. *DNA Analysis* (Solving Crimes with Science). Broomall, PA: Mason Crest Publishers, 2014.

Kiesbye, Stefan. *DNA Databases* (At Issue: Civil Liberties). Detroit, MI: Greenhaven Press, 2011.

Krapohl, Donald J., and Pamela K. Shaw. *Fundamentals of Polygraph Practice*. San Diego, CA: Academic Press, 2015.

Kroener, Inga. *CCTV: A Technology Under the Radar?* Farnham, UK: Ashgate, 2014.

Roberg, Roy R. *Police & Society*. 6th ed. New York, NY: Oxford University Press, 2015.

Saferstein, Richard. *Forensic Science: From the Crime Scene to the Crime Lab.* 3rd ed. Boston, MA: Pearson, 2016.

Smith, Brad. *K9 Tactical Operations for Patrol and SWAT*. Eggleston, VA: Wolfe Media Resources, 2013.

Suen, Anastasia. *Careers with SWAT Teams* (Extreme Law Enforcement). New York, NY: Rosen Publishing, 2014.

Young, Tina, and P. J. Ortmeier. *Crime Scene Investigation: The Forensic Technician's Field Manual*. Upper Saddle River, NJ: Pearson/Prentice Hall, 2011.

INDEX

F

facecam systems, 65–66
facial reconstruction, 83
Federal Bureau of Investigation (FBI), 73
fingerprinting, 56–59
firearm identification, 79–81
firearms, 32, 34, 40–45, 79–81, 91
FirstNet, 22–23
flash-bangs, 45
foot patrols, 10, 13–14
forensic analysis, 71–89, 91
forensic anthropology, 83, 84–85
forensic art/illustration, 88
forensic botanists, 10, 87
forensic computing, 89
forensic engineers, 87
forensic entomology, 83–86
forensic odontologists, 86–87
forensic pathology, 82–83

G

Galton, Francis, 57, 58
Goddard, Calvin, 79

H

hair and fiber analysis, 71–74, 91
helicopters, 17
Henry, Sir Edward R., 58

I

Interpol, 26

J

Jeffreys, Alec, 61, 62

L

Landsteiner, Karl, 76
latent fingerprints, 58, 69
Lattes, Leone, 76
lie detectors, 50–52
Locard, Edmond, 67, 69
luminol, 69

M

Mauser, Peter Paul, 43
mobile digital terminals (MDTs), 24
motorcycle patrol, 14, 16
mounted patrols, 13–14
mug shots, 24, 55
multishot revolver, 42